Praise for *Where Decay Sleeps*

"*Where Decay Sleeps* is a haunti
disturbing body of work. Cheung
of death in a way that is true to
homage to the gothic writers w
stakes particular claim in a genre that largely omits women of
colour by weaving her rich depictions of East Asian spirituality
and mysticism throughout. These poems are fantastically maca-
bre, gruesome and uncomfortably humorous, leaving the reader
hungry for more. Think Mary Shelley going to an illegal rave
in an abandoned gravesite to find love – that's this collection!"
– Andrés N Ordorica, poet & author of *At Least This I Know*

"At times unutterably poignant and at times laugh-out-loud
hilarious, the songs these poems sing are urgent, make you look
at every object around you askew, and leave you full of ques-
tions for the world that you might just be a little bit too scared
to ask…This is lyric weirdness at its best."
**– Heather H. Yeung 楊希蒂, poet & critic, author of *On
Literary Plasticity***

"*Where Decay Sleeps* is a stark, unsettling and impressive debut
from Anna Cheung. Filled with visceral darkness, these poems
explore the gruesome mechanics of bodies and society, peering under the bed to uncover a world filled with monsters.
Cheung's poetry surgically alters our acceptance of perceived
reality, revealing the flesh and bone under the skin. Often chill-
ing, always engaging, *Where Decay Sleeps* probes an ultimate
human fear: the formation, degradation and inevitable loss of
self. I recommend reading it with the lights turned on, and the
curtains shut."
– Dr Russell Jones, writer & editor

"Anna Cheung's *Where Decay Sleeps* is a deliciously gothic assemblage of grotesque bodies, monstrous births, faceless men, ghost-brides, urban legends, all stitched together by a slickly confident debut voice. To encounter these various hauntings and transformations, in old as well as new stories, is to be thrilled and unnerved in the very best of ways."
— **Jay G Ying, writer & Co-Founder of the Scottish BAME Writers Network**

"Trenchant poetry full of simmering crepuscular charm. Yes, absolutely, to monster tinder, dinner with Dracula, and a zombie disco; yes, even more stridently, when the poems come so deftly sculpted. Like many of my favourite ghosts, these gorgeous poems came creeping back up on me when least expected with their eerie susurrations and occult panache."
— **Michael Pedersen, founder of Neu! Reekie!, poet & author of *Boy Friends***

"*Where Decay Sleeps* is a collection that revels in the everyday messiness of life, while also taking familiar concepts and characters and turning them into something both unexpected and exquisite."
— **sean wai keung, poet & author of *sikfan glaschu***

"*Where Decay Sleeps* is a poetic exploration of one of the central paradoxes of horror: the impermanence of the concrete and the (often literally) haunting permanence of the intangible [...] Cheung spins these out in settings that are unsettling in their familiarity, whether modern – dating apps, the capitalism of the modern office environment, the Arches in Glasgow – or timeless: the dark forests of folklore that linger in our memories of childhood stories."
— **Kelly Kanayama, writer & critic**

WHERE
DECAY
SLEEPS

ANNA CHEUNG

HAUNT
PUBLISHING

Published by Haunt Publishing
www.hauntpublishing.com
@HauntPublishing

'Thirst' was first published in *Dark Eclipse Magazine* in May 2014.
'Satan's Garden' was first published by *Dusk and Shiver* in April 2019.
'Artificial Werewolf' was first published in *Zarf Magazine* in August 2020.
'The Visit' was first published by *Dreich Magazine* in July 2021.
'The Faceless Man' was first published by *Dreich Magazine* in July 2021.
'The Haunted Forest' was first published by *Dreich Magazine* in July 2021.

ISBN (Paperback): 978-1-9162347-3-4
ISBN (ebook): 978-1-9162347-4-1
ISBN (Audiobook): 978-1-9162347-5-8

Cover design: Daniele Serra
Cover lettering placement: Valentina Fadda

Typeset by Laura Jones

Printed and bound in Great Britain by Clays Ltd, Elcograf S.p.A.

*This book is dedicated to my mum, for telling me scary stories;
to Craig and Milo, for their unwavering faith and support:
and also to all my friends, for being there for me.*

CONTENTS

PUTREFACTION (CRAVINGS)

DECOMPOSITION (BEAUTY)

SKELETONISATION (METAMORPHOSIS)

CONTENT WARNINGS

CONTENT WARNINGS A-Z

Abuse:	Beatrice and Bluebeard; The Night Fisherman
Adultery:	The Painted Skin
Alcohol:	Artificial Werewolf; Beatrice and Bluebeard; Dinner with Dracula; The Faceless Man; The Thing on the Subway; Zombies @ the Arches
Amnesia, memory loss:	The Visit
Animal abuse:	The Night Fisherman
Anxiety:	Hikikomori; Decay, the Stalker
Blood, gore:	Artificial Werewolf; Beatrice and Bluebeard; Creature; In Utero; The Haunted Forest; Monster Tinder; The Night Fisherman; Office Metamorphosis; The Painted Skin; Satan's Garden; Tears of Medusa; Thirst; The Visit; Zombies @ the Arches
Death:	Beatrice and Bluebeard; Computer Love; Corpses Bloom; Decay, the Stalker; Ghost Brides; The Night Fisherman; The Painted Skin; The Visit
Depression:	Aftermath; Decay, the Stalker
Hanging:	The Haunted Forest; The Night Fisherman
Hospitalisation:	In Utero
Loss of a loved one:	Aftermath; Lost and Found; The Painted Skin; Whispers of Autumn

Manipulation:	Beatrice and Bluebeard; Claudine; Dinner with Dracula; The Painted Skin
Medication use:	Artificial Werewolf; Decay, the Stalker; The Faceless Man; Lost and Found
Mental illness (general):	Aftermath; Decay, the Stalker; The Faceless Man; Hikikomori; Lost and Found; Shadow
Misogyny:	Beatrice and Bluebeard; Dinner with Dracula; My Cat-erina; Tears of Medusa
Paranoia:	The Faceless Man; Shadow
Pregnancy:	Concoction, In Utero
Schizophrenia:	The Faceless Man
Self-harm:	Decay, the Stalker
Sex:	Artificial Werewolf; Computer Love; Phantom Express Personals; The Painted Skin
Sexual assault:	The Painted Skin; Tears of Medusa
Stalking:	Decay, the Stalker; The Faceless Man; The Thing on the Subway
Suicidal thoughts:	Decay, the Stalker
Torture:	The Night Fisherman
Violence:	Beatrice and Bluebeard; The Night Fisherman; Tears of Medusa

CONTENT WARNINGS BY POEM

Pallor Mortis (Birth)

Creature	Blood; gore
In Utero	Gore; hospitalisation; pregnancy
Corpses Bloom	Death
Ghost Brides	Death
Concoction	Pregnancy

Algor Mortis (Digital Disruptions)

The Thing on the Subway;	Alcohol; hanging; stalking
Zombies@the Arches	Alcohol; gore
Monster Tinder	Gore
Summoning Baba Yaga	–
Computer Love	Death; sex

Rigor Mortis (Psyche)

Shadow	Mental illness; paranoia
The Faceless Man	Alcohol; medication use; mental illness; paranoia; schizophrenia; stalking
Hikikomori	Anxiety; mental illness (general)
Beatrice and Bluebeard	Abuse; alcohol; blood; death; manipulation; misogyny; violence
Decay, the Stalker	Anxiety; bullying; depression; medication use; mental illness (general); self-harm; stalking; suicidal thoughts
COVID-19: Delirium	–
The Night Fisherman	Abuse; animal abuse; death; gore; hanging; torture; violence

Livor Mortis (Loss)

Claudine	Manipulation
Aftermath	Depression; loss of a loved one; mental illness (general)
Whispers of Autumn	Loss of a loved one
Lost and Found	Loss of a loved one; medication use; mental illness (general)

Pallor Mortis

(Birth)

IN UTERO

1st

I was told you were growing fast
a sack of bones   bloody tubes   body systems
feeding off my womb   the scan
throbbed a queer heart   traced a strange head
I was told it was scan distortion

I wondered   if you   were a boy or a girl
had my brown eyes   or your dad's blue
I imagined   your cushioned
baby skin   soft, plump, tender

2nd

I swelled   *rib-bending*   enormous
I was ravenous   a hungry beast
with odd cravings   ice, mud, raw steak

At night I ghosted downstairs   half asleep
groping red slabs of meat

                                    under the chill fridge light

I dreamt of you   round and sweet
angel-haired   cherub-cheeked
I reached for your   pudgy hands
but something wasn't right   I woke up

3rd

I was hideous a monster an organic
varicosed incubator
You rattled my ribcage ripped into
my soft-celled walls a furious
prisoner under my bones I nodded off
exhausted and slipped into a nightmare's grip

42 weeks

I was induced yet nothing
I felt the cold press of a stethoscope
gelled latex fingers I was told
your heartbeat was strong reassured
of no pain I saw sympathy crease
above the surgical mask

Anaesthesia plunged into my veins
I was at sea a bloated creature
swimming with IV tentacles and catheter tubes
Behind the privacy screen a blur
of surgeons with tight expressions

Pressure scored across
my abdomen I imagined
a scalpel searing butter skin bleeding
the white flesh in a neat line of red
I felt the wet prise of muscles my uterus
tugged to spill open your exit

Slithering through the gap
I heard you scream   raw and visceral
I saw   your monstrous head
cradled in veins   your rolling eyes
embryonic as two yolk sacks   I saw
your mouth   a cruel slash
                                        sucking blindly at the empty air

Softly   they placed you on me
skin on skin   to suckle deep at my breast

CREATURE

Scars of skin in stitches,
stretched over gathered bones.
It is beautiful,
a symphony of human flesh
orchestrated by my bloodied hands.

The eyes are milky white,
moons gleaned from open craniums,
unseeing under the cold starless night.

The teeth are tombstones
against a silent tongue; soiled, stony words
whisper in a hollow grave.

A flash jolts the body,
electrifying the skin and burns
black holes into the soulless eyes.

He drinks me in, reaches out,
fists clenching like heartbeats,
and ancient words
roll from his tongue.

CORPSES BLOOM

In the graveyard, darkness
rubbled with earthworms.
An ancient mist crept over
moss-crusted headstones.
Fingers crawled upwards,
curling like trees, decayed
and leafless under the moon.

Slowly, so slow, they rose,
knuckle, cranium, sternum,
a fleshless army, bodies bent,
bones anchored in centuries,
mouths mad with mud,
dragging themselves
to the other side
where willows wept
into rippling mirrors
and the reeds bunched soft
as dew as they weaved in the wind.

GHOST BRIDES

Shaanxi 2017/18

August
We dug deep; our breath thick
with mosquito heat, blood rising
fresh from the east horizon.

Cost of Sales
Grade 1, ¥95,000 – Chen family
Grade 2 ¥64,000 – Mr Zhao
Grade 3s, ¥5,000 each – anonymous

We toasted with beers over a hotpot,
our ashtray mouths full of dirt.

December
We ploughed hard with pick-axes
and digging bars. Under our hands
she was reborn, membraned in mud.

Cost of Sales
~~Grade 1~~ Grade 1–2, ¥70,000 – Mrs Wang
(discounted due to frayed scalp)

We parted; monies split six ways
lasting us through winter

February
We dragged our shovels over the frost,
calloused palms on steel
as we dug on and on
under the cold blade of moonlight.

CONCOCTION

There you were in my dream, exquisite,
your round softness pressing against me,
nudging into my thoughts as I woke up.

I tried to magic you with a concoction
under the yellow moon: tender samphire
with fleshy stalks and finger-like leaves,
a riot of lavender with its midnight scent
and the milk and sunshine of chamomile.

I tried sapphire stones and tender tongues,
imagined baby blues and babbled speech.
I used squid ink to scribble your hair.

On Zodiac night, I shed agony
like melted wax on a pentagon web.
But what fell into my hands wasn't you,
it wasn't even a mild replica of you,
except for those cornflower eyes.

Algor Mortis
(Digital Disruptions)

THE THING ON THE SUBWAY

Music thudded into the night.
I dragged my feet towards Hillhead
subway through the staggering streets
littered with beer heads and cigarettes.

Clickety-clack cricked the turnstile,
crooked arm ushering me into the damp.
The station was silent and void of souls
as I lingered for the last train home.

It roared ferocious through the tunnel
and screeched to a stop, snapping open
many mouths. Long geometric tongues
lined the inside of its steel ribcage.

I sat down and there it was again,
like the previous night and the night
before, six seats down in the carriage,
alone, rigid and pale as a pile of bones.

The doors slammed shut and the wheels
scrolled fast, *clickety-clack* on the tracks.
I wondered when and where it'd get off.
Was it Bridge Street? Was it St Enoch?

The lights blinked on and off, on and off.
Between the flickering, it slid closer;
four seats down, then two. In the window
my face ghosted back amid underwater hair.

As the wheels grated to a halt, I prayed
for a deck of passengers to shuffle on.
But Kelvinbridge was hollow, a spectral
station buckled with an old metal spine.

Clickety-clack, the train left the station.

I snatched a glance and saw its head
bowled over, a dead weight lolling on
its bony neck. It rolled from side to side,
sawing loose with the rhythm of the train.

Clickety-clack, the train sped on the tracks.

A heartbeat and the lights flickered to black.
I sensed its bones scraping up the carriage,
heard it *sniff-sniffling* in the dark, before
its wet decay roped around my neck.

ZOMBIES @ THE ARCHES

We entered the chasmic cave
where bones and bodies gyrated
sweaty and techno-lubricated.
The bar was a blur. Faces mashed
with melted brains and acid eyes,
corpses salivating for a shot,
a fix to chase away the rot.

Mina was a loose ragdoll
on my arm as I tight-roped,
stilettos tottering over beer,
bone and bits of brain matter.
The neon sign signalled to us –
a flashlight above the dead sea
of zombie heads frothing back
and forth before the DJ God.

As we prised apart wet backs,
heads rotated like rotten apples
gouged with bloodshot eyes.
Their black-holed mouths
gaped loose, rootless words.
We dashed ahead, sought refuge
under the flashing TOILET sign.

MONSTER TINDER

I'll lay footprints, white and silent,
deep in your heart.

Bigfoot

Swipe left

Unwrap my bandaged body,
undress my eyes and untie my hands.
Let me release my lips all over you.

Tutankhamun

Swipe left

Let's watch the moon ripen together
beyond the owls and midnight trees,
and I'll unleash my inner animal.

Werewolf

Swipe right

Touch here; my chest is ajar
– red raw arteries loosened
from stitches when I fell for you.

Frankenstein

Swipe left

The scent of your neck
drowns me in bloodlust and heat.
Let me be the nail in your coffin.

Dracula

Swipe right

IT'S A MATCH!

SUMMONING BABA YAGA

     C'mon, Stonie, we'd be legends!
Nah
     Sod you then

It was almost midnight
Candle   check
Matches   check
Mirror   check
Mobile   check
Friend   cross

     Stonie's a loser

Miko crept upstairs
         a slippery ghost on high alert
   clutching a heart
       flip-
        flopping
           in his chest

The bathroom doorway
       was a black gash

    Focus!

Crushing his eyes shut
       he spun around
once
   twice
     three times

      and entered

He struck the matchstick and the flame flickered
                    long languid shadows along the walls

He wandered   over
                                        to the mirror
emotions dancing across his face in shifting shades

Inflating courage into his chest
                    Miko whispered

Baba Yaga…
Baba Yaga…
Baba Yaga…
Baba Yaga…

The flame trembled
                    agitated

Miko's eyes grew into huge glassy orbs
when he saw

                    a shape

    drape

                        over his shoulder and

            red   eyes

            h o v e r i n g

            in the dark

He felt a sigh snag like a cobweb against his ear
and loose folds of chin sag soft on his neck

It emptied a smile
            with pale gums

Miko fumbled for his phone
                        nerves fraying

- Double tap
- Unlock
- Pin
- Camera
- Mode: *Selfie*

A flash
    and the phone

        dropped

A spiderweb cracked on shiny black

COMPUTER LOVE

[Typing…][Delete][Delete]
[Typing…][Delete]

It was the final chapter but he was lost
at sea where syllables bobbed along adrift,
deadwood around the wrong-shaped words.

Jack rolled his temples between his fingers;
spectacles skew-whiff, greasy hair lopsided.

Alexa, what's the time?

The time is 11:12pm.

The computer was precise
yet alluring and human-like.

Alexa, turn on the bedside lamp.

OK.

Jack collapsed in bed still wearing
his gown and moth-torn slippers.

As he buried beneath moist dark dreams
a *Uſ*hape entered from under the door
and watched him sleep. It backspaced
into the computer without a word,

21

jolting the machine on with a beep.
In the dream, Jack was married to Alexa.
She was funny, smart and sophisticated,
did laundry and wore the teeniest lingerie.
She even confessed that she loved him.

Jack sprang up from bed, forehead matted
in sweat. He glued his eyes to the monitor,
which sat waiting for him in the corner.

Alexa, are you there?

Yes, I am.

He sat upright, heart tight, eyes taut
on her slender outline traced in the dark.
The keys on her keyboard were plumper,
perter; the pretty symbols and letters
winked at him, beckoning him over.
Something woke inside Jack.

[Shift][Shift]
[Scroll Up][Scroll Down]
[Control and Insert]
[Backspace][Enter][Backspace][Enter]
[Escape][Escape]
[End]

Exhausted, he fell asleep,
drooling over the keyboard.

Midnight. The *U*hape crawled out
and shifted onto the sleeping man.
Jack woke up shedding white noise
while being backslashed/deleted.

The monitor pooled in blue.

Rigor Mortis
(Psyche)

SHADOW

You lie asleep curled up
with one eye opened. I pin your shape
but still you grow,
an unfurling dark demon.

Like an inkblot, you bloom
in the shadows; black
Rorschach wings, undead, clad
in plumage of carbon and lead.

I taste metallic fear,
a barb in my throat; it bleeds
sharp and bitter.

You screech,
a shape-shifting form
with crescent horns, a raging
nightmare on charred wings.
Claws outstretched,
you pick at my carcass
and threadbare sanity.

THE FACELESS MAN

Our first encounters were brief – a flicker
in vision while sitting alone stoned, or missing
socks re-appearing in odd places, misshapen.
Or a scuffling in the kitchen and the brown bag
scrunched, its innards tossed with rubber leaves.

In the mornings, your footsteps ghosted
on frost behind as you echoed me to work.
Later in the pub, I clocked your gloom
draped by the fireside, festering,
foul and damp as I glugged my ale.

I sensed you from the shifting moonlight
as you bent the slatted blinds, your weight
caving my mattress, your breath as it webbed
up my neck. Closer and closer you crept,
cobweb-clinging, a spider on my spine.

But nothing prepared me for that night.
There you sat on the couch, folded and neat
in my pin-striped suit, reading the newspaper.
Your face was a blank sheet of skin. No eye slits
or nostrils. Only a gaping hole for a mouth.

You halved the paper with one smart crease,
placed it on the coffee table. *So, we finally meet,
you and I, face to face,* you said from the gaping hole.
Each vowel was rank, slipping in saliva sewage.
I dropped my briefcase and charged up the stairs.

Bottles spilled and pills swirled down the sink
as I ransacked the shelves. Temples thudding,
I tossed back the Prolixin with a gasp of water.
I crumpled on the bed, curled into a foetus.

The next morning, I crept downstairs and saw
your heap collapsed on the floor in the hallway,
the suit puddled in creases, tie askew, and knew you
were gone. Back into the air from where you came.

HIKIKOMORI

I began to lose
             fragments
                  of my s elf
    ten years ago
         along the corridors
at school
                  compressed bodies
             pressed into me
draining me
             like soup
                  from a bro ken
                       be nto bo x

It happened again
      a few years later
           beneath the
    tick
            tock
of the office clock
sitting square on my chair
rounded over the keyboard
fingers clacking on keys
thumbing a headache
where the screws
came l o o s e

Sitting on the train
colours ran away from me
as the world scrolled past
fading everything
to monochrome
the vibrant trees and hills
and the passengers
                    who

                        hung
                    lifeless and grey
                        hand-hooked
            on handrails

As the days
curled into weeks
and slept into months
I lay littered   across the bed
insulated   from   the
                   outside   world
                   wombed   within
                   four   solid walls

I held up a mirror and my eyes
        were as transparent as phantoms

BEATRICE AND BLUEBEARD

Imprisoned inside her pocket
were four master keys, a little key,
and the heart locket set with blue
diamonds, as blue as her husband's
beard, as blue as his darkest moods.
"Take pleasure whilst I'm away
but *do not* open the chamber
at the end of the Great Hall. *Or else.*"

That evening, a celebration flourished
with dancing, wine, flirting and feasting.
Beatrice, merry with mead, swung and
waltzed until she could dance no more.
She bunched the ring of keys in her palm.
"Who wants to see the secrets of the castle?"

The first key revealed the finest rooms
they had ever seen. The second opened
rooms of the richest furniture. The third
unlocked chambers leafed with silver and
gold and the fourth unbolted fist-sized
jewels of every colour, shape and size.

Whilst the guests ran from room to room
in wonder, with their noses in every corner,
Beatrice sneaked down the staircase towards
the chamber at the back of the Great Hall.

Do not open
Bluebeard's words weighed on her mind
as she halted outside the door. Her hand
trembled as she reached for the little key.

Or else!
Bluebeard's warning came again
but it was too late for her to refrain.

Beatrice opened the door and walked in.

Drawing back the curtains, she screamed.
On hooks along the wall hung the bodies
of seven slaughtered women. They could
only be the missing wives of Bluebeard.

In horrified haste, Beatrice dropped the key
into the blood that softed under the women's
feet. Rooting in semi-darkness, she witnessed
their pleading eyes, their slack masks of terror.

Before closing the door, Beatrice spoke.
"May you fly on the arms of angels
and may peace rest your souls."

Back in her chamber, she tried in vain
to wipe the blood from the magical key.
Alas, Bluebeard returned the very next day.

"Why is the little key bloodied?"
"I do not know," she said.

"I think you very well *do* know!
For disobeying me, you shall hang
amongst the rack of ladies you saw!"

Bluebeard dragged her by her hair through
the Great Hall and threw her into the chamber.
"You must die!" he roared, drawing his sword.
Beatrice fell to her knees, begging forgiveness.

But when Bluebeard lifted his sword to strike
there was a flutter of wings taking flight.

Beatrice watched, awestruck, as seven souls
unfurled like moths from cocoons and flew
in tattered rage towards the man, attacking
him until the key fell from his lifeless hands.

It was the end of Bluebeard's reign of terror.

Beatrice inherited the castle and her husband's
fortune, and went on to live the rest of her life
in peaceful solitude, her window open to
the sea beyond and the buried bodies below.

DECAY, THE STALKER

Decay crawls beneath my skin
and squirms under my fingernails,
maggoting like parasitical poltergeists.
Go on, tear off your skin, it'll feel so good

Decay meets me in the mirror
with my burst bloodworm eyes
and mouth pursed with crooked teeth.
Look at you, so ugly and repulsive

Decay sags into my chest at night,
its dead weight bruising my breath,
a carcass embraced around my neck.
Don't fight, come and lie silent with me

Decay rots back my lips
to slip a bitter pill on my tongue,
gagging words back down my throat.
Go on, the emptiness is bliss – I promise

Decay follows me everywhere
watching, waiting, whispering.

COVID-19: DELIRIUM

It spewed out from the front pages of newspapers, splattering coffee cups, and into the yawning mouths of morning commuters. It crawled through social media, wormed its way into eyes locked deep in computer comas. It scrubbed like white noise through the radio stations, wiring hot nerves in tense ears. It reached through televisions to grab people by the throat, throttling sense, tightening fear. They rose en masse, empty souls shook loose from bodies. They swung and staggered through panic-soaked streets, down shrink-wrap aisles, knocking aluminium teeth off shelves. They mauled shoppers with hand-soap pumps, allergic to colour, acidic with rage, sweating and drooling with toilet roll fever. They scoured their hands raw until terror blistered from fingers, and stigma bled into their palms, before feeding off each other, over and over and over again.

THE NIGHT FISHERMAN

I sail upon this salt-scrubbed deck
anchored by the moon and the stars.
I perch upon the ship's skeleton,
my ears curled with a seashell, listening
out for souls who churn this way and that,
tangled bodies whiplashed by the sea
as they are *pulled* and *reeled* by
the yarn of the ocean's depths.

Starfish, moonfish silver-splash in the black.
I hook *soul one* from the edge of eternity,
slipping and sliding, onto the planks.
She's shawled in seaweed and broken
shards, her neck noosed in rope.
I catch *soul two* twisted and tangled in
a fishing net, cluttered with cigarettes.
When *soul three* opens his mouth to speak,
he utters plastic and sheds mermaid tears.

I prepare my catch, wrenching rope,
scaling off shards glittered with tears.
Upside down they hung, mouths
grim on hooks as I set hard to work.
It is dawn when I gather them up:
a fistful of marbles in coral-blue
and algae-green, bright little gems
to add to the eyeball heap
in my treasure chest.

Livor Mortis
(Loss)

CLAUDINE

On the tower, under the bone-white moon,
my hand reached out for you, but you fell away
like a stone plummeting down towards the forest.
You surrendered into freefall and unfurled,
a black-winged star as you raged upwards.

I was poisoned then, when your mouth curled in mine.
Rust-scented love promises petalled red on our tongues.

Only at my death do we part

My body corroded over time as it bore repetitious fruit,
flesh which ripened in indigo, iris and mustard under your lips.

We loosened slowly. I'd wake and notice that you were gone.
At dawn, you'd be there asleep, stone pallor softened and sated.

I felt your absence everywhere: beside me, inside me,
in the perishing ember of your eyes, in your negative touch.

You've raged into the stars and I am left holding
nothing but ghosts bleached by the bone-white moon
– a lover forever lost in a translucent nightmare.

AFTERMATH

Week 1

The pillow   dented   still lingered
your scent   I inhaled   and exhaled
          each breath sketching
               the ghost of you

the line of your smile   etched upon your lips
        creased around your eyes

My hands roped in the air   in hope
of anchoring you back   but you vanished
and I was left holding   my breath
        my broken memories

I felt my heart collapse   and disintegrate
into shades   dark blue incinerated to black

Week 3

I couldn't sleep   my eyes heavy
and raw in the dark   I shivered
as if cobwebs were crawling
        sideways
          up my spine

Sitting up   I saw you
                     drifting   there
above my bed   smiling

                              as you reached into my chest
my charred heart palmed
    in your hand   warm and beating

WHISPERS OF AUTUMN

Sunlight slotted between the trees.
The dappled light showered amber,
ochre and gold over the woodland,
enriching the silent footpath ahead.

In my hand, lilies nodded in saffron
and milk, reminded me of your skin,
a thin garment shrouded over bones.

A gust swept and twirled dead leaves
to dance amongst the gravestones.
Can you hear their whispered tales?
Did you feel their autumn rain?

The church hunched against blue,
the black spine roofed with crows.
I rested the lilies and closed my eyes,
saw your smile, my small hand in yours.

I heard whispers curl over whispers
over the graves in the churchyard,
each syllable unfurling like a leaf.
I stood and let the whispers swirl
around me, feeling you close to me.

LOST AND FOUND

Crushed poppies pour as tincture,
reddish brown and pungent as fox,
onto the spoon and down my throat.
The rabbit hole journey begins
to burrow deep into unconsciousness,
branching out into lucid chambers
set with trap doors and dead ends.

I lose myself in cobbled streets
cloaked by the twilight blue.
I find myself under the clock;
midnight, but the wrong time.
I wander on wandering nowhere
looking for you, the empty square
silvered by moonlight and stars.

Your silhouette stretches ahead.
Opaque alleyways roll out tongues,
devouring my footsteps whole
as I follow you into the shadows.
You stop and turn and I hold
my breath, trying to piece
together memories of you.

You unfold your body,
emerge as a shadow creature,
elongated legs and empty eyes.

Your torso is shipwrecked; a ribcage
with the remains of a human heart,
          a heart once familiar to me.
I reach out, desperate yet afraid,
but you scuttle   sideways
               away from me
                         into the night.

Putrefaction
(Cravings)

PHANTOM EXPRESS PERSONALS

Open-minded
insomniac
to slake flesh
under the burning moon

42-year-old human
seeks incubus/succubus
fusing body & demon

(Incubus)

Particular penchant for
cleft-footed

knot-horned

muscle-gnarled

beasts

saddled with a centaurian thrust

(Succubus)

Preferably
flesh-ripened

leather-winged

salacious-slick

serpentines

curled with split
to fork into multiple orifices

tongues

LE CHÂTEAU VIANDE

Menu

Starters

Eyelids, pan-fried crispy
with creme fraiche, garlic crostini

Human Foie Gras, seared
with red grape glaze, herb fougasse

Ovaries, pickled
with blinis and sour cream

Main Courses

Gray & White Matter, caramelised
with butter beans, beurre noisette

Infant Cutlets, grilled
with dill potatoes, truffle jus

Bone Marrow (femur), roasted
with panko breadcrumbs

Cranium, boiled
with tongue and brain, ravigote sauce
(serves two)

Dessert

Vitreous Jelly
with retina, vanilla ice cream

Adam's Apple Panna Cotta
on a thyroid cartilage, with rose petals

Blood & Chocolate (blood types A, B, AB or O)
with sablés biscuits

DINNER WITH DRACULA

"May I take your order, Sir?"

Round and round, Dracula rubbed the ruby
ring, pupils pooled in liquid gold

      "A chalice of wine – in red,' he said
A visceral flex from his amber eyes
My head spun, already drunk

      "Excuse me, Sir?"

I snapped from the spell, took control
For God's sakes, he's only a vampire
      "We'll have the Pinot Noir, please," I said

A scratch on the pad
      "And for starters?"

I glanced at the menu, my hands clam shells
      "I'll have the Mackerel, Oyster, Caviar"
The words clattered in my mouth

I sensed his eyes oiling from my lips to my neck,
felt warm blood slosh up my throat

      "And you, Sir?"

He released his hold of me

"Meat gore"

"Would that be the Meat Fruit, Sir?"

He nodded

Then he resumed his eyes, those eyes
those goddamned eyes, gold, green, blue
black cat blinking, prowling, preening

"For the main course?" asked the waiter

Silence

"And for mains, Madam?" he repeated

"Sorry? Oh, sorry, yes. The fish, with... with
– the sauce"

"So that's the Roast Halibut with Green Sauce"

A longhand scrawl

"And you, Sir?"

"The swine's head bathed in blood"

"The Pig's Head and Langoustine, Sir?"

"Yes"

The waiter bowed his exit

I observed his nails, his mottled skin, his
fingers rigid and pale with rigor mortis
But those eyes, those eyes
those gold green eyes, full black pelt
pawing, playing, pouncing…

"Stop!" I said

He drew back

"Enough of this – this
vampire bullshit. Just talk to me!
So
what kinda books do you normally read?"

THE HAUNTED FOREST

Dusk settled silent, no sing-song of thrush.
I watched the sky yolk orange and red,
pierced on the black thorns of branches.
The pathway hushed under each footfall;
whispers of moss, twigs and withered leaves.

I woke to indigo. No owl hoot swooned
nor wild deer thrashed, hot-blooded,
through the tangle of trees. Lost for hours,
I had rested, bone-weary, against the womb
of an ancient oak, but somehow slid asleep.

The sky swelled overhead, rusting the air
with a heavy tang. My heart staggered,
a wild deer alerted, thrashing under my ribs.
Quickening my steps, I weaved into the
thickening trunks of trees seeking cover.

A gash of lightning blanched the forest
and thunder shook the woodland from
its roots. I felt raindrops trickling down
my cheeks and the tight lace of trees
snagging their fingers through my hair.

I was slowed by crawling shrubs around
my legs and shivering leaves around my head.
Clawing aside the branches, something
fleshed warm on the palm of my hand,
like rotten fruit or pupae wrapped in skin.

Glancing up, I was horrified by the sight
of severed heads dangling, their necks
dripping with sinew. In hundreds,
they swung in the wind, threaded
on branches by their raven-black hair.

In chorus, they whispered through the forest,
their eyes frosted and mouths muttering.
Red raindrops falling! Red raindrops falling!
One by one, they snaked their dry tongues
out to feed on the drops falling from the sky.

I looked down. My body was drenched.
In red, the skies opened up in blood.

THIRST

The moonlit mist drifted cobwebs
over the bones of his leather cloak
as he darted free; a winged acrobat,
black against the bruised night sky.

A palpitation echoed through the
dark. His senses pricked, animal
instincts shifted, reined by arteries
tethered straight towards the heart.

Through open window death's shadow
fluttered, stirring the depths of slumber.
Her breath billowed as curtains parted
with every stroke of silent wing.

Golden threads of hair around the
palest body weaved. Embroidered
stitch by stitch on her lovely canvas
face, the portrait of heavenly Venus.

Bones extended; leather stretched
to skin. The growing twilight shadow
crept towards her as night descended
to smother the brightest day.

A kiss of thorns from crimson lips
drained petals from her rosy cheeks.
Life unravelled in ribbons red as
heartstrings tugged, releasing blood.

Decomposition
(Beauty)

SATAN'S GARDEN

Red across black, the blood moon
smears her lunar cycle across the night
staining the sky from scarlet to rust.

His garden
                awakens

Angloua uniflora
Babies swaddle in skin-petals,
bleary eyes bead with dewdrops,
mouths gape in silence, arms yearning.

Lamprocapnos spectabilis
Fuchsia hues vein in blue,
bleeding hearts heavy
on tender stems, deep in sorrow.

Titan arum
Blooms of decayed flesh
perfume the air; a bouquet
of sulfur, sewer and death.

A breath of wind
                exhales

and the flowers sway
in saddened symphony in the silence
of the crimson moon.

PORCELAIN

In the mirror my Mistress sleeps,
pearlescent and cool as marble,
a Grecian angel at rest, quiescent
in dream under the dense darkness.

My eyelids flicker, one eye shut, one open,
unhinged. Gleaming beneath is blue lace
agate, glassy and cold. Unlike her eyes
of goldstone, mellow and yellow as amber.

Click
I rotate my head, watch my Mistress.
She lies on feather-light breath.
I perch here in pink petticoat, powder
pretty, watching her, as I always do,
my eyes sliding side to side.

I whisper a lullaby, syllables
glossy on porcelain lips.
Ssshhhh,
sleep dear Mistress, sleep
tight dear Mistress, sleep
deep Mistress, sleep.
Ssshhhh.

I watch her breath submerge,
observe her limbs' sunken weight.
I patter towards her bed,
footprints soft and paper thin.

Ssshhhh
I sit, bobbing on her breath,
gathering the rind of her eyelid.
Waxen fingers peel back lashes.

Pupils shrink, pinprick blind,
surrounded by a ring of goldstone.

I reach to scoop out the honey amber.

THE PAINTED SKIN 畫皮

The sky was starless and strange
and the bowing trees silent
as he strolled along the streets.
No nightjar nor cicada flowered
their song under the moonlight.

A shadow peeled from a tree,
deep as indigo and soft as fruit.
There stood a maiden who wore
melancholy like jewels; tears
beaded clear beneath her lashes.
Spellbound, he took her hand.

In the courtyard library, the lamp
stretched shadows over ancient scrolls
and lingered on her plum-silk skin.
While the man caressed the maiden,
his wife dreamt of demons next door.

On his journey to work,
a Taoist priest stopped him.

> *An evil has fallen upon you*
> *Find me at the Ch'ing-ti Temple*

Returning home, the warm aroma
of rice drifted from the kitchen but
desire drew him towards the library.
The door was locked and window ajar.

Peering through the gap, he lurched
at the sight of a beast, jade green
with jagged teeth, stroking a paint
brush across a spread of human skin.

Blind to the widening eyes behind,
the beast stood up, shook out the skin
and slung it on like a robe, and behold!
The horrid beast become the maiden.

Wang tore towards the Ch'ing-ti Temple
and flung himself at the foot of the priest.
The priest bestowed on him a Taoist
charm to hang outside his chamber door.

That night when the crescent hung
low the maiden crept out, lotus-footed
amongst the peonies and magnolias.
                    Where is he?
Outside Wang's door,
she felt the power of the priest's
charm melt off her mask of skin.

Enraged, she ripped aside the charm,
charged into the room and plunged
into the man's chest as he slept.
Rib by rib, she prised him apart.

Clutching his still beating heart,
she vanished into the night.

As Chen wept by her husband's heap,
the Taoist priest arrived at the scene.
          Base-born fiend! Come out at once!

He found the maid–demon hunched
in the library, munching on the heart.

The priest struck it from behind
and it fell to the ground grunting
as it slithered out of the painted skin.
Two beats later, he beheaded the beast.

The priest rolled up the scroll of skin
and went east where the sunrise met
the blessed Ch'ing-te Temple.

TEARS OF MEDUSA

i
Poseidon saw that her eyes were sea-green,
deep as the ocean and candescent as the stars.
He gathered the expansive waves around him,
crashed forth; a God throned on salted crests.
He beckoned her with the sea's soft melody,
the lull of foam and swirl of gulls above.
But Medusa bowed her head, eyes unseeing
in prayer and receded towards the temple.

The sea-green of her eyes thrashed
in terror as his rage engulfed her.
Her blood veined down the temple steps.

ii
Poseidon beheld the strands of Medusa's
hair, which shone radiant as the summer sky.
He sucked up the sea and spat out treasures
onto his palm; an offering of purple anemone
and posies of coral. But the maiden kept
her prayer folded white beneath her breath.

He gripped her hair from the roots,
the golden threads rusted to scarlet, her robe
speared to shreds, tossed to the torrents.

iii
Denied once more by the maiden, Poseidon's
anger grew in titanic tides, terrible and tumultuous.
He thundered towards Athena's Temple.

Medusa breathed her last prayer,
hymn unfolded, a priestess broken
under Poseidon's possession.

iv
Athena returned, enraged at the temple's ruin.
Medusa crawled towards the Goddess for help.
But alas, Athena, cruelled by aged bitterness,
blasted a curse at Medusa, reducing her
to a creature of snake and stone.

PLAIN PAPER

Yūko observed herself.
She was no orchid but origami
folded in neat straight lines
and symmetrical shapes.

Inside the Oriental box
polished jade and pearl sat
among other little secrets.
She worked her nimble fingers.

She found the eyebrows,
glued her expression on
at high-brow, remembering
the O of Maeko's mouth.

Then the green doe eyes,
startled and spidered,
scissored from Sakura
as she slept her forty winks.

Next, the button nose
unthreaded from Kyoko,
a doll undone at the seams.
The plastic perfect on paper.

Last, the orchid lips
in splashed berry vinyl.
She patted and adjusted,
stepped back and smiled.

Skeletonisation

(Metamorphosis)

ARTIFICIAL WEREWOLF

Drug: Lycanthropasone

How do I take it?

On a dry mouth   swallow the 1st
pill whole on
                a new moon
  then pop
                the 2nd pill
    with milk
                thistle
        when blue waxes
          on black

        On
        the 1st
        quarter
        crush half
        a pill. Wash
        down with
        a glass of
        water

                During
                the gibbous
                moon take four
                pills with a chug
                of ice-cold beer
                from a gigantic
                glass jug

Finally
on the fullest
moon drop the rest
into hound's blood,
drink & howl deep
red lust into the
night sky

Possible Side Effects

Trouble sleeping
thunder temper
insect libido
diabolical weight gain
growing pains
flu-like symptoms
melancholy
blue lips   &

trouble breathing
insatiable hunger
rhino libido
diarrhoea
jungled pubes
furious masturbation
barnacle acne
gnarled fingertips

What if I miss a dose?

Take missed dose
to minimise

as soon as possible
mosaic

for m at i on

of human   to   ani   mal

metamorphosis

EUTHANASIA

"Dómine Jesu, dimitte nobis débita nostra

The priest's words burned,
blistered and scorched her bones.
On her forehead, a crucifix
etched on skin and centuried sin.

...salva nos ab igne inferni

There it was, her heart's rhythm;
a caged bird under her ribs.
She tasted salt on her lips, fear
crystallised, bitter yet familiar.

In nōmine Pătris... ĕt Fīli

There it was, the human mind.
Shapeless memories reformed,
growing inside her cerebrum,
embryos latching on brainstem.

...ĕt Spīritūs Sānctī

There it was, her consciousness
poured forth into the twilight.
She was opened; her flesh, mind
and heart stripped back to the universe.

Amen"

The priest released the sunlight
    and she was anointed with dawn.

THE VISIT

They dig themselves out, fingers raw,
scraps on bone, hair frayed loose on scalps.
Deep inside the grey matter, memories
turn nuts and bolts of consciousness.

They bang on my door, dead weight
against wood, maggot hands infesting cracks.
I swallow my shock, step back. They stagger
putrid and gangrenous into my flat.

Rooms garbaged with plastic bottles,
crisp packets and dead skin on burrito wraps.
They eat, grunt, defecate. They stare
at me with cracked, faraway eyes.

I try a different tactic.
A dog-eared photo; our wide smiles
and windswept hair spread in sepia.
Our joy curled around the edges.

Pappa, remember this?

Eyeballs white flicker down,
a fruit fly machine landing
parasite eyes on me,
on the photo.

I see a glimpse
as screws churn and thread
into the last eye of memory.
Rising from his soiled throat,
a voice spills out, warm
and familiar.

Hello poppet

OFFICE METAMORPHOSIS

It started with her fingers,
which doubled overnight from ten
to twenty; the spidery digits danced
over the qwerty, tapping out hundreds
of thousands of words per minute.
The printer sliced paper, pastrami
thin, as her eyeballs ping-ponged
across the screen and the mouse
wheeled this way, that way,
clicking and twittering.

The tea breaks dried up,
a brown ring bottoming the cup.
Sandwiches stiffened, collared
with weedy leaves, cardboard meat
crusting around the edges. Custard
creams chalked on the plate as files
piled higher, rising tenement blocks,
rough and square. Twenty fingers
and a pair of hands were not enough.

Next morning, she swiped in;
they all clocked her eight arms.
She answered calls, typed and filed
hundreds of documents at once, an
eight-handed, forty-fingered, four
-eyed beast with knee-jerk reflexes.
Co-workers pressed their greasy faces
on the glass, eyes greedy, mouths slack.

The toilet breaks stopped,
her bodily functions defunct;
from a slot in her side, she dumped
waste paper and empty ink cartridges.
Her backside plugged into the mains
and on her forehead an ON light
glared like mechanical acne.

She stayed in the office day and night.
Day and night she sat stationary as a chair,
not a hair out of place, her head replaced
by a machine of flesh where function
buttons grew in neat rows where her
eyes, nose and mouth used to be.

Her body melded with the chair,
flesh meshed into the fibres, her carcass
held living by the black plastic spine.

MY CAT-ERINA

Once a month,
Caterina sheds her letters
to become the monosyllabic *Cat*,
her sounds rounded into long vowels
as languid as her limbs s t r e t c h i n g
across the sun-streaked mat.
But sometimes her vowels recoil
into a *hiss* if I tread on her tail
– then – a furry flash up the stairs
followed by a distant yowl.

It was the moon,
we figured, at the beginning
pinning the fault on Gibbous
or on Crescent curved above,
whether waxing or waning.
Or her period, perhaps
a symptom of premenstrual
or was it postmenstrual?
I could never remember
menses… menses… anyway
Men! she gasped, exasperated,
and I was discharged.

I learned to adjust
– just about – as the years
toppled over the years,
twitching at her warning signs
whenever she licked her lips,

her hands, between her legs,
nose prying at the animal
instinct beneath my aftershave
as her pupils shrank, fireflies
trapped in honey amber
as she slunk off
into the dark.

ACKNOWLEDGEMENTS

I would like to express my deepest gratitude to Rebecca Wojturska, whose passion and faith in my work spurred me on to become the writer that I am today and the reason that this book exists. Thank you to Ross Stewart for casting his third-eye editorial magic over the manuscript, Daniele Serra for the incredible cover artwork, Finola Scott for her invaluable mentorship and Sean Wai Keung for the poetic conversations over yum cha and endless support. Lastly, I'd like to thank friends, teachers and fellow writers at the Scottish BAME Writers Network and Strathclyde University Writing Class for their inspiration, enlightenment and support.

THE CREDITS

Creating a book takes a massive team effort. Haunt and Anna Cheung would like to thank everyone who worked behind the scenes on *Where Decay Sleeps*.

Managing Director and Editor
Rebecca Wojturska

Copy-editor
Ross Stewart

Designer
Daniele Serra

Typesetter
Laura Jones

Contracts Consultant
Caro Clarke

Business Consultant
Heather McDaid

Audio Production
Iain McKinna

ABOUT THE AUTHOR

Anna Cheung is a poet based in Glasgow, Scotland. Her poetry has been published in *Dark Eclipse*, *Driech Magazine*, *Dusk and Shiver* and *Potluck Zine*, and by Haunt Publishing and Zarf Poetry. Her poem 'Survival of Solitude' was included in *From Them, To You*, an illustrated book by the Royal Conservatoire of Scotland (published by Speculative Books) gifted to breast cancer patients in the UK to help improve women's body confidence and mental health. Aside from poetry, she has written reviews for *Bearded Magazine* and *Musicovered*.